KU-314-564

MASTERPIECES IN THE VICTORIA & ALBERT MUSEUM

CROWN COPYRIGHT RESERVED

LONDON: HIS MAJESTY'S STATIONERY OFFICE
1952

FOREWORD

By SIR LEIGH ASHTON, F.S.A.

DIRECTOR OF THE VICTORIA AND ALBERT MUSEUM

IT is appropriate to issue an album of masterpieces in the year marking the centenary of this Museum; for it was in 1852 that the Museum of Ornamental Art was set up in Marlborough House—a small collection of works of applied art which was destined to become one of the world's outstanding collections of fine and applied arts of all countries, periods and styles.

In 1857 the Museum of Ornamental Art was merged with a new collective museum of science and art assembled on part of the South Kensington site. This ground had been bought by the Commissioners of the 1851 Exhibition to further the Prince Consort's plans for a great cultural centre of museums and colleges in the district. This new museum was opened as the 'South Kensington Museum' by Queen Victoria on 22 June, 1857.

The art collections, from their small beginnings, grew faster than any of the other sections, until they came to occupy all the present site of the Victoria and Albert Museum—the scientific exhibits being transferred to the west side of Exhibition Road and elsewhere. As these collections expanded, the ideals of the original Museum of Ornamental Art were broadened: they had been described as the 'application of fine art to objects of utility' and 'the improvement of public taste in design'. To these were now added the manifold tasks of selecting, describing and preserving for their own sake the finest products of artistic craftsmanship.

By the end of the century the Museum—in its art collections—had grown to include fine and applied arts of every kind, although the exhibits represented chiefly European art since classical times, together with the arts of the Near and Far East. By this time the scholar, the student and the general public were all catered for by a great and complex organization which was still growing rapidly.

New buildings had been added from time to time and finally, in 1891, a competition was held for designs to cover the areas fronting on Exhibition Road and Cromwell Road and so complete the general architectural scheme. It was won by Mr. (later Sir) Aston Webb. However, the foundation stone of this final section was not laid until 17 May, 1899. It was the last public ceremony performed by Queen Victoria, and she directed that the title of the Museum be changed to 'Victoria and Albert Museum'. On 26 June, 1909, King Edward VII opened the new buildings and at the same time the title 'Victoria and Albert Museum' was confined to the art collections only, the scientific collections being given the new name 'Science Museum'.

The basic arrangement of the art collections from 1852 until 1945 was by materials and types of object; the names of the Departments were: Architecture and Sculpture; Ceramics; Engraving, Illustration and Design; Library and Book Production; Metalwork; Paintings; Textiles; and Woodwork. These Departments, with those of Circulation and Extension Services, still determine the administrative and academic organization of the Museum. But after the Second World War, I decided that there should be a radical alteration in the arrangement of the galleries. A new and well-informed public has been steadily growing in this country and the arts have come to play a very important role in both the education and the private lives of countless men and women. Half the Museum is now devoted to displaying the evolution of the historic styles, with objects from all departments, brought together in a series of specially arranged galleries. This series of galleries forms what are called the Primary Collections. There are also, in the Primary Collections, special galleries devoted to Islamic Art, Far Eastern Art and the National Collection of British Water-Colours. The arts and crafts of India are kept together in the Indian Section in Imperial Institute Road.

The rest of the Museum is devoted to the Study Collections, which are arranged according to the Museum Departments described above.

I feel that this re-organization enables the Museum to carry out its educational function more efficiently, and to provide greater attractions for the general public, while at the same time safeguarding the interests of the scholar.

The present album is arranged on the basis of the Primary Collections. When looking at the 225 objects illustrated in this book—in quantity a mere fraction of the Museum's exhibits—one realizes the remarkable achievement of a century's scholarship and expertise. It reflects not only the high standards of taste and appreciation of three generations of museum officials, but the wisdom and generosity of countless private collectors who have given or bequeathed their treasures to the Nation.

I hope this album will find its way into many institutions and many private hands, and that it will make a real contribution to the enjoyment and understanding of the visual arts.

September
   1951

VIEWS IN THE PRIMARY COLLECTIONS

GOTHIC ART

ITALIAN RENAISSANCE ART

CONTINENTAL ART, 1570–1820

ENGLISH DECORATIVE ARTS, 1660–1750

ENGLISH DECORATIVE ARTS, 1660–1750

ENGLISH DECORATIVE ARTS, 1750–1820

NOTE: The illustrations in this album are arranged approximately in the order of the Primary Collections as described in the Foreword.

EARLY MEDIAEVAL ART

1. THE SYMMACHORUM DIPTYCH. Ivory. Roman; late 4th century

2. TAPESTRY-WOVEN PANEL. Silk. Egyptian; 4th–5th century

3. HERMES. Woollen pile. Egyptian; 4th–5th century

4. THE ALTON TOWERS DIPTYCH. Ivory. Early Christian; 5th century

5. A WINGED MONSTER. Silk. Sassanian; 6th–7th century

6. HERO AND LION. Silk. Alexandrian; 6th–7th century

8. THE MIRACLE OF CANA. Ivory.
Alexandrian; 6th century

7. THE EASBY CROSS. Sandstone. English;
7th–8th century

9. THE EASBY CROSS. Detail

10. THE LORSCH GOSPELS. Book-cover. Ivory. Carolingian; 9th century

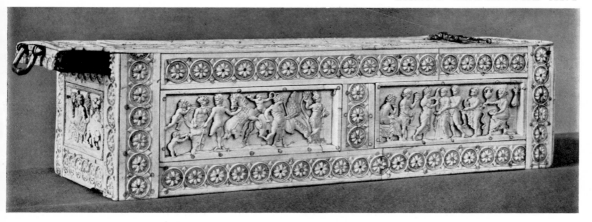

11. THE VEROLI CASKET. Ivory. Byzantine; 8th–10th century

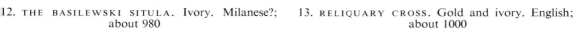

12. THE BASILEWSKI SITULA. Ivory. Milanese?; about 980

13. RELIQUARY CROSS. Gold and ivory. English; about 1000

14. THE SION GOSPELS. Gold and enamel. North French or German; 10th–12th century

15. PASTORAL STAFF. Ivory. English; 11th–12th century

16. THE VIRGIN AND CHILD. Ivory. Byzantine; 10th–11th century

17. THE GLOUCESTER CANDLESTICK. Gilt bell-
metal. English; about 1110

18. THE ADORATION OF THE MAGI. Whalebone. English;
beginning of the 12th century

19.

20.

21.

19. SAINT JOHN THE BAPTIST. Ivory. Byzantine; 11th or 12th century

20. THE DEPOSITION. Ivory. Spanish; 11th–12th century

21. EWER. Bronze-gilt. Mosan; early 13th century

22. THE ELTENBERG RELIQUARY. Copper-gilt. Rhenish; second half of the 12th century

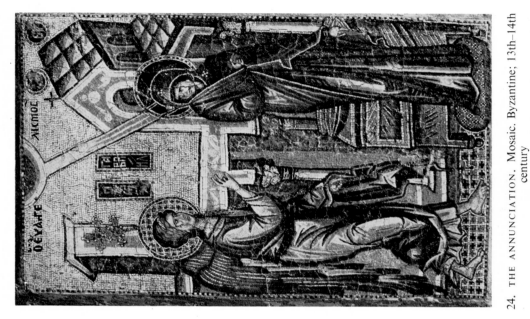

24. THE ANNUNCIATION. Mosaic. Byzantine; 13th–14th century

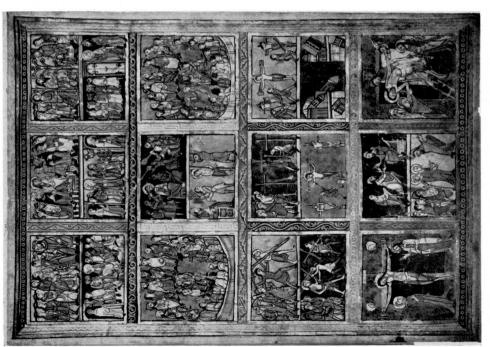

23. PSALTER. English; first half of the 12th century

NORTHERN GOTHIC

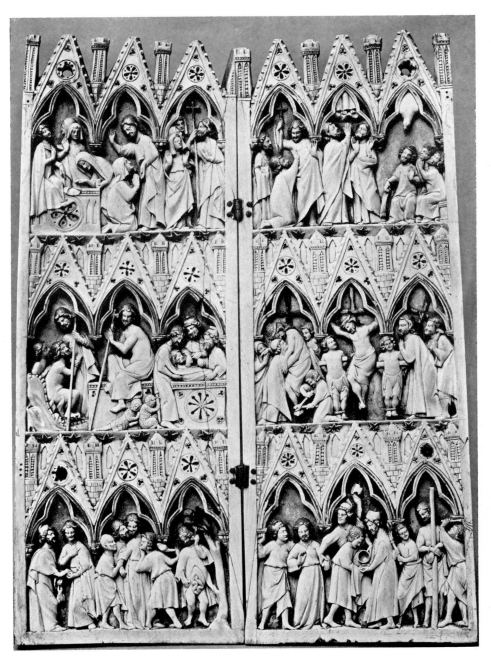

25. THE SOISSONS DIPTYCH. Ivory. French; end of the 13th century

26. THE JOHN OF THANET PANEL. Embroidery. English; early 14th century

27. THE CLARE CHASUBLE. Embroidery. English; second half of the 13th century

28. THE STUDLEY BOWL. Silver-gilt. English: late 14th century

29. THE VALENCE CASKET. Copper-gilt. French; 1290–96

31. THE VIRGIN AND CHILD. Sandstone. French; early 14th century

30. THE TWO MARIES AT THE SEPULCHRE. Ivory. French; mid 14th century

32. THE MÉRODE CUP. Silver-gilt. Flemish or Burgundian; early 15th century

33. THE RAMSEY ABBEY CENSER. Silver-gilt. English; second quarter of the 14th century

34. THE VIRGIN AND CHILD. Ivory. French; beginning of the 14th century

35. THE REICHENAU CROZIER Copper-gilt. South German; 1351.

36. DIPTYCH. Ivory. English; early 14th century

37. THE SYON COPE. Embroidery.
English; early 14th century

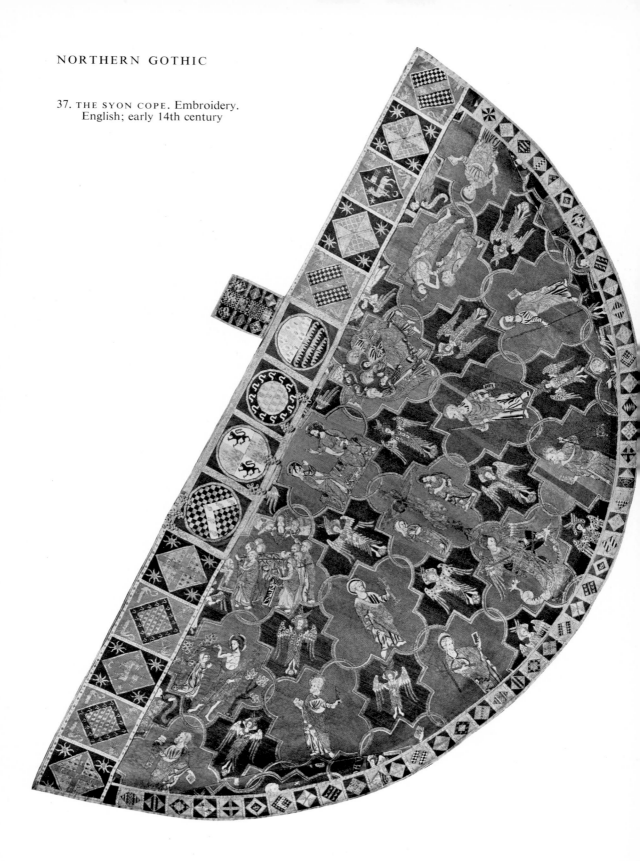

38. THE WINCHESTER COLLEGE WINDOW. Stained glass. English; about 1400

40. THE ST. DENIS MISSAL. French; about 1370

39. THE ANGEL OF THE ANNUNCIATION. Oak. French; 15th century

41. THE TROJAN WAR. Tapestry. Burgundian; about 1470

42. THE DESCENT, THE ENTOMBMENT AND THE RESURRECTION. Tapestry, Franco-Burgundian; early 15th century

43. WILD MEN. Tapestry. Swiss; mid 15th century

44. SUSANNA AND THE ELDERS. Tapestry. Flemish; about 1500

SPANISH GOTHIC

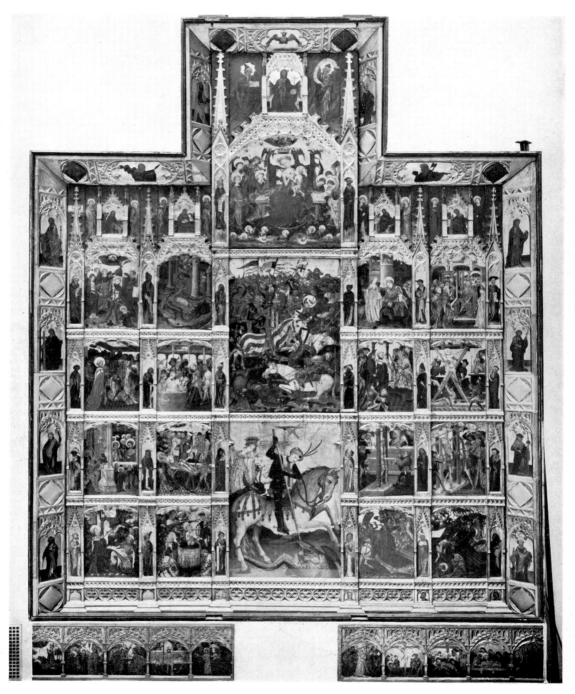

45. THE RETABLE OF ST. GEORGE. Painting on wood. Spanish; about 1400

46. DISH. Tin-glazed earthenware.
Spanish; first half of the 15th
century

BOWL. Tin-glazed earthenware.
nish; first half of the 15th century

49. CARPET. Wool. Spanish; late 16th century

48. CIBORIUM. Silver-gilt. Spanish; late 15th century

ITALIAN GOTHIC

50. THE ANNUNCIATION. Marble. Florentine; about 1290

51. CASKET. Painted wood.
Bolognese; second half of the
14th century

52. THE ANGEL OF THE ANNUNCIATION.
Wood. Pisan; mid 14th century

53. THE ARCHANGEL GABRIEL. Marble.
Pisan; about 1275

54. THE CORONATION OF THE VIRGIN. Tempera painting by Nardo di Cione (fl. 1343–66).
Florentine

57. THE VIRGIN ANNUNCI-
ATE. Terracotta. Florentine;
second quarter of the 15th
century

56. CHASUBLE. Embroidery. Florentine; first quarter
of the 15th century

55. MADONNA AND CHILD. Terracotta. Florentine; about 1425

59. CHALICE. Silver-gilt. Venetian; about 1480

58. THE NATIVITY. Gold engraving under glass. North Italian; late 14th century

60. THE VIRGIN AND CHILD. Istrian stone. By Bartolomeo Buon. Venetian; 1451

61. THE EXPULSION FROM EDEN. Glazed terracotta. Florentine; second quarter of the 15th century

62. MARRIAGE CHEST. Painting on gesso. Florentine; early 15th century

63. DISH. Tin-glazed earthenware. Florentine; about 1450

64. DRUG-POT. Tin-glazed earthenware. Florentine; second quarter of
the 15th century

ITALIAN RENAISSANCE

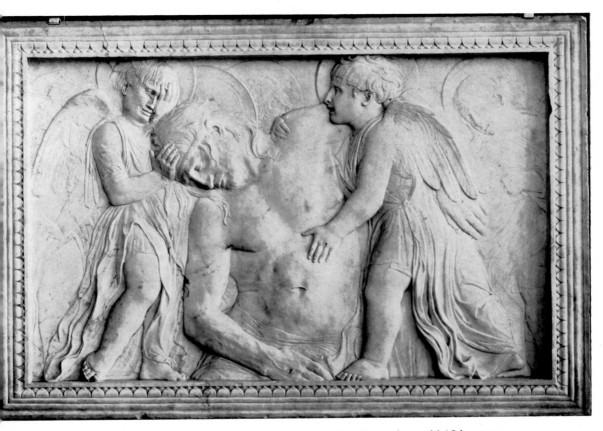

65. CHRIST IN THE TOMB. Marble. By Donatello. Florentine; mid 15th century

66. THE ASCENSION. Marble. By Donatello. Florentine; about 1430

66a. DETAIL: HEADS OF APOSTLES

66b. DETAIL: FIGURE OF CHRIST

68. THE VIRGIN AND CHILD. Marble. By Desiderio da Settignano. Florentine; third quarter of the 15th century

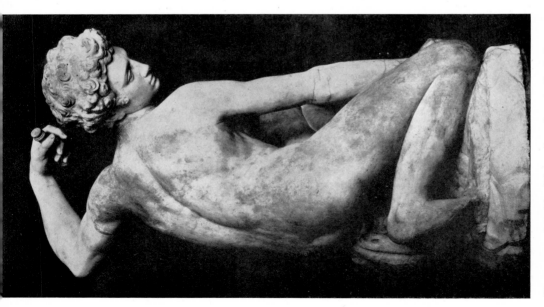

67. CUPID. Marble. Florentine; first half of the 16th century

69

70

71

72

73

69. HERCULES. Bronze. By Bertoldo di Giovanni. Florentine; last quarter of the 15th century

70. CUPID. Bronze. By Donatello. Florentine; second quarter of the 15th century

71. THE LAMENTATION. Bronze. By Donatello. Florentine; 1450–60

72. THE CANNING JEWEL. Pearl. Tuscan?; late 16th century

73. SLAVE. Wax. By Michelangelo. Florentine; about 1516

74. STEMMA. Enamelled terracotta. By Luca della Robbia, Florentine; 1460–1470

74

75. THE VIRGIN WITH THE LAUGHING CHILD. Terracotta. By Rossellino.
Florentine; about 1465

76. GIOVANNI CHELLINI. Marble. By Rossellino. Florentine; 1456

77. THE VIRGIN AND CHILD. Tempera painting. By Crivelli (1430?–95). Venetian

78. ALTARPIECE. Marble. By Andrea Ferrucci. Florentine; about 1495

79. CHRIST LED FROM JUDGMENT. Wax. By Giovanni Bologna. Florentine; about 1575

80. AN ALLEGORY OF DISCORD. By Francesco di Giorgio Martini. Sienese; last quarter of the 15th century

81. HORSEMAN. Bronze. By Il Riccio. Paduan; early 16th century

82. SATYR AND SATYRESS. Bronze. By Il Riccio. Paduan; about 1512

83. MARRIAGE CHEST. Painting on gesso. Sienese; about 1475

85. ILLUMINATED MANUSCRIPT. North Italian; about 1470

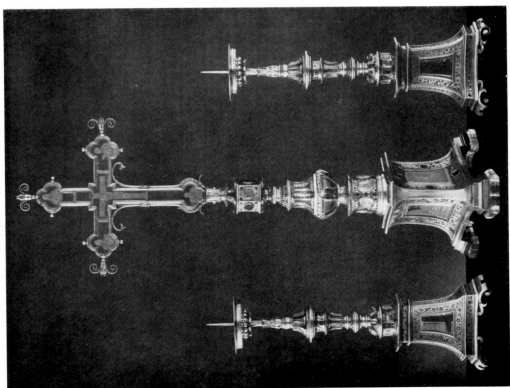

84. CRUCIFIX AND CANDLESTICKS. Crystal and silver-gilt. North Italian(?); about 1520

86. THE MIRACULOUS DRAUGHT OF FISHES. Cartoon for tapestry. By Raphael. Rome; 1515

87. THE ADORATION OF THE
MAGI. Enamelled gold. Spanish;
16th century

88. THE MARTELLI MIRROR. Bronze.
Florentine; early 16th century

DIES

MAIVS

89. MAY. Enamelled terra-cotta. By Luca della Robbia. Florentine; 1440–45

90. PLATE. Tin-glazed earth-enware. Castel Durante; about 1515

91. CHIMNEY-PIECE. Sandstone
By Desiderio da Settignano. Florentine; mid 15th century

92. THE VIRGIN AND CHILD
WITH ANGELS. Marble. By
Agostino di Duccio. Florentine
about 1460

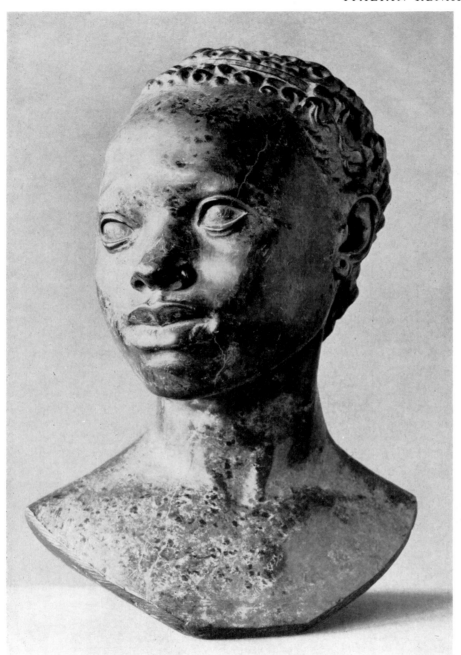

93. HEAD OF A NEGRESS. Marble. Florentine; late 16th century

94. HENRY VII. Painted terracotta. By Torrigiano. Italian (Florentine); early 16th century

NORTHERN RENAISSANCE

95. RUSTIC SPORTS. Tapestry. Flemish; early 16th century

96. A CASTLE WITH THE
ADORATION OF THE MAGI.
Silver-gilt. French; late 15th
century

97. ST. MARGARET IN PRISON
Stained glass. Flemish; 1520–

98. THE RESURRECTION. Tapestry. Flemish. First quarter of the 16th century

101. THE VIRGIN AND CHILD. Boxwood. By Veit Stoss. German; 1500–10

100. SIDEBOARD. Walnut. French; about 1560

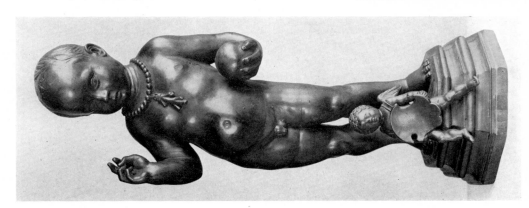

99. THE CHRIST CHILD BLESSING. Bronze. By Labenwolf? Nuremberg; early 16th century

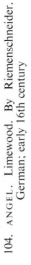

104. ANGEL. Limewood. By Riemenschneider. German; early 16th century

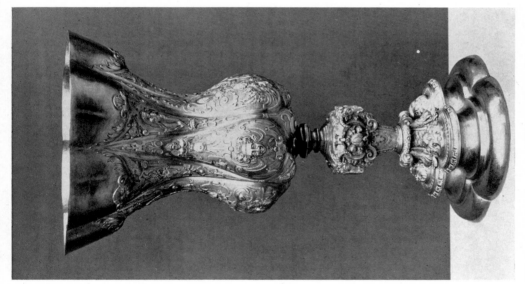

103. COLUMBINE CUP. Silver. Nuremberg; about 1572

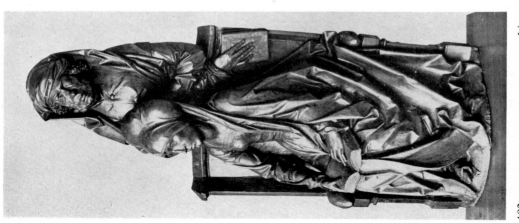

102. MARY SALOME AND ZEBEDEE. Lime-wood. By Riemenschneider. German; about 1506

105. THE LOUIS XII TRIPTYCH. Painted enamel. Limoges; about 1500

106. QUEEN CLAUDE OF FRANCE. Painted enamel.
By Léonard Limousin. Limoges; about 1550

107. MARIE DE'MEDICI. Chalk drawing.
By Rubens. Flemish; about 1617

108. BOOK COVER. Enamelled gold. South German; about 1600

CONTINENTAL ART

109. MR. BAKER. Marble. By Bernini. Rome; about 1639

110. NEPTUNE AND GLAUCUS. Marble. By Bernini. Rome; about 1622

111. THE VIRGIN OF SORROWS. Painted wood. By Pedro de Mena. Spanish; mid 17th century

112. CHARLES II. Marble. By Pelle. French; 1684

113. THE JUDGMENT
SOLOMON. Silver tazza
Adam Van Vianen. Du
1612

114. COMMODE. Marquetry. French; early 18th century

115. DIANA. Boxwood. By Leonhard Kern. German; mid 17th
century

116. SEATED GIRL. Lead. By Adriaen de Vries.
Netherlandish; first quarter of the 17th century

117. A HUNT PICNIC. Porcelain. By Bustelli.
German; 1759–60

118. A BACCHANTE. Terra-
cotta. By Marin. French; 1786

120. COVERED BEAKER. Glass. Engraved by Spiller.
German; about 1700

119. LOUIS XV. Terracotta. By L. S. Adam. French; about 1741

122. AUTUMN. Porcelain. By Kaendler. Meissen; about 1765

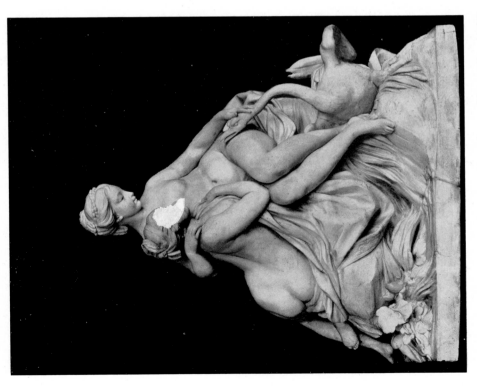

121. LEDA AND THE SWAN. Porcelain. By Falconet. Sèvres; about 1765

123. MADAME DE POMPADOUR. Oil painting. By Boucher. French; 1758

124. VOLTAIRE. Marble. By Houdon. French; 1781

126. UPRIGHT SECRÉTAIRE. Marquetry and or-molu. By Roentgen. Franco-German; end of the 18th century

125. SECRÉTAIRE-TOILETTE. Marquetry and ormolu. French; about 1775

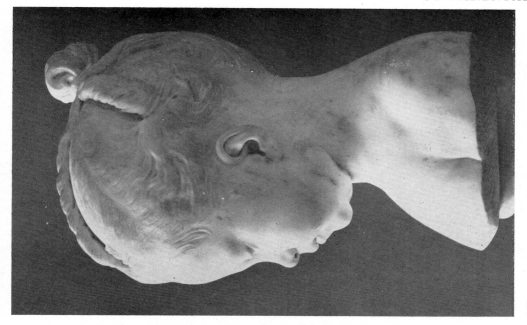

128. ALEXANDRINE D'ETIOLLES. Marble. By Saly. French; about 1750

127. THE DUKE OF REICHSTADT. Portrait miniature. By Isabey. French; about 1820

129. COMMODE. Marquetry. By Roentgen. Franco-German; 1780–90

130. RIVER-GOD. Terracotta. By Clodion. French; end of the 18th century

ENGLISH ART 1500–1660
TUDOR & EARLY STUART

131. THE GREAT BED OF WARE. Oak, carved, painted and inlaid. English; last quarter of the 16th century

133. PRINCE ARTHUR'S CUPBOARD. Oak. English; about 1500

132. TABLE DESK. Painted leather. English; about 1525

136. THE HOWARD GRACE CUP. Silver-gilt and ivory. London; 1525-6

135. THE MOSTYN SALT. Silver-gilt. London; 1586-7

134. THE VYVYAN SALT. Silver-gilt. London; 1592-3

137. QUEEN ELIZABETH. Portrait miniature.
By Isaac Oliver. English; about 1600

138. THE ARMADA JEWEL. Gold set with
precious stones. English; about 1588

139. ANNE OF CLEVES. Portrait miniature. By
Holbein. English; about 1539

140. MRS. PEMBERTON. Portrait miniature.
By Holbein. English; about 1540

141. THE SIZERGH CASTLE ROOM. Oak inlaid. English; about 1575

144. YOUNG MAN AMONG ROSES.
Portrait miniature. By Hilliard. About 1588

143. GOBLET. Engraved
glass. English; 1581

142. YOUNG MAN AMONG FLAMES. Portrait miniature. By Hilliard. English; late 16th century

145. REBECCA AT THE WELL. Plate, silver-gilt. London; 1573–4

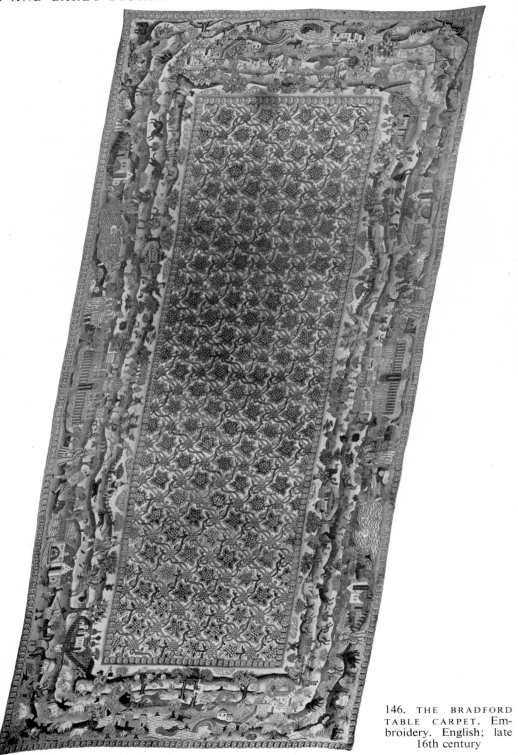

146. THE BRADFORD TABLE CARPET. Embroidery. English; late 16th century

147. COURT CUPBOARD. Oak. English; early 17th century

148. RICHARD SACKVILLE, THIRD EARL OF DORSET. Portrait miniature. By Isaac
Oliver. English; 1616

149. THE FLIGHT INTO EGYPT. Tapestry. Sheldon; late 16th century

150. THE GODS DISCOVERING MARS AND VENUS. Tapestry. Mortlake; about 1625

151. THE ADORATION OF THE SHEPHERDS. Embroidery. By Edmund Harrison.
English; 1637

ENGLISH ART FROM 1660

152. THE STONING OF ST. STEPHEN. Limewood. By Grinling Gibbons. English; late 17th century

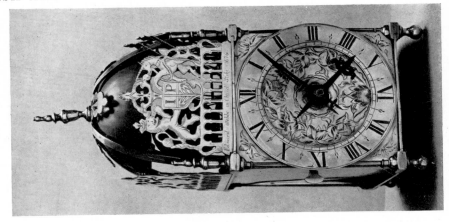

155. CLOCK. Silver case. By Edward Webbe. English; 1676

154. A HERALD. Chalk drawing. By Lely. English; late 17th century

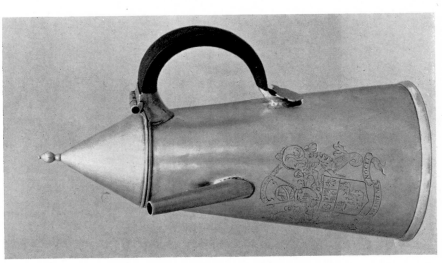

153. TEAPOT. Silver. London; 1670–1

158. THE ASHBURNHAM GARNITURE.
Silver-gilt. London; 1675–6

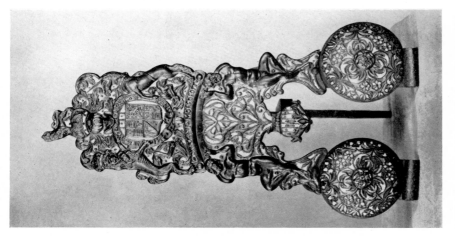

157. FIREDOG. Enamelled brass. English;
second half of the 17th century

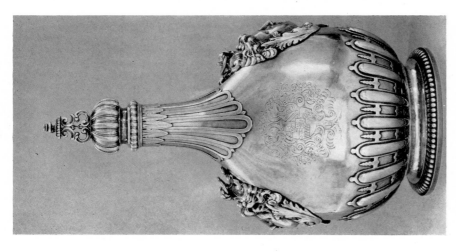

156. PILGRIM-BOTTLE. Silver. By Pierre
Platel. London; 1702–14

159. THE STERNE CUP. Sil
ver-gilt. London; 1673–4

160. SALVER. Silver-gilt.
Thomas Farren. London
1733–4

161. CABINET. Walnut with marquetry. English; about 1700

162. CHINOISERIES. Tapestry. By John Vanderbank. Soho; early 18th century

163. SIDE-TABLE. Carved and gilt wood. By Flitcroft. English; 1725–6

164. CHEST. Carved and gilt gesso. English; about 1720

165. THE GARRICK FURNITURE. Japanned wood. By Chippendale. English; about 1775

166. THE KIMBOLTON CABINET. Rosewood and satinwood. By Adam. English; 1771

167. LIBRARY TABLE. Mahogany. English; about 1755–60

168. COMMODE. Mahogany with marquetry. By John Cobb. London; about 1775

169. SETTEE. Carved mahogany. English; about 1755

170. BEDSTEAD. Japanned wood.
By Thomas Chippendale. English;
1750–55

171. THE NEWDIGATE CEN-
TREPIECE. Silver. London;
1743–4

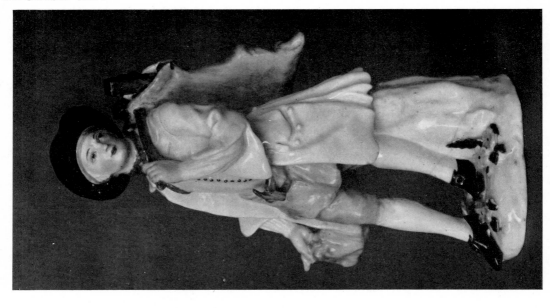

174. THE CARPENTER. Porcelain. Chelsea; about 1755

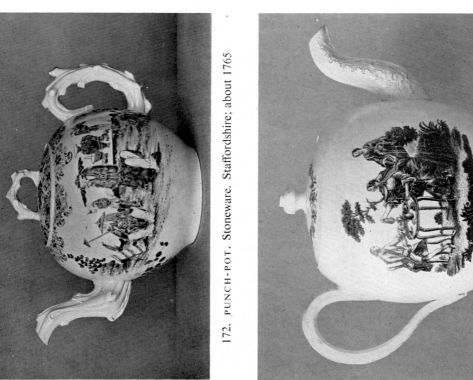

172. PUNCH-POT. Stoneware. Staffordshire; about 1765

173. TEAPOT. Earthenware. Burslem; about 1765–70

175. THE MUSIC LESSON. Porcelain. Chelsea; about 1765

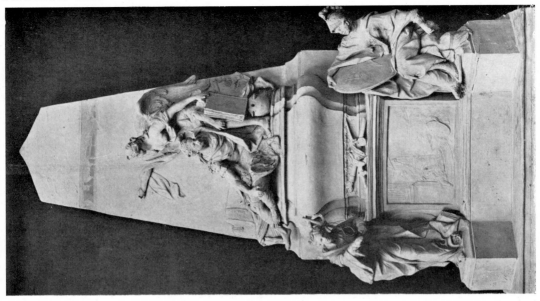

177. MODEL FOR THE MONUMENT TO JOHN, DUKE OF ARGYLL. Terracotta. By Roubiliac. English; 1745

176. SIR GEORGE SAVILE. Marble. By Nollekens. English; 1784

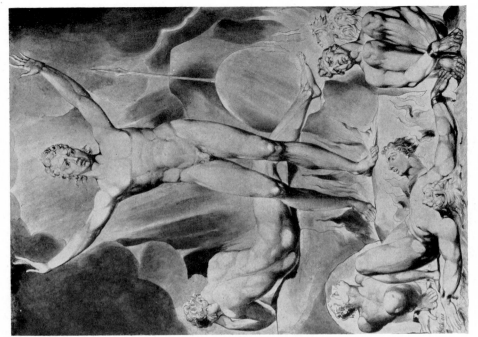

179. SATAN AROUSING THE REBEL ANGELS. Water-colour.
By William Blake (1757–1827)

178. IN A SHOREHAM GARDEN. Water-colour. By Samuel Palmer
(1805–1881)

180. GLOUCESTER, 1840. Water-colour. By Peter de Wint (1784–1849)

181. LANDSCAPE WITH RIVER AND CATTLE. Water-colour. By John Sell Cotman
(1782–1842)

182. ENTRANCE TO THE MALL, SPRING GARDENS. Water-colour. By Thomas Rowlandson (1756–1827)

183. THE PAINTER'S TWO DAUGHTERS. Oil. By Thomas Gainsborough (1727–88)

184. KIRKSTALL ABBEY, YORKSHIRE—EVENING. Water-colour. By Thomas Girtin
(1775–1802)

185. THE HAY WAIN. Oil. By John Constable (1776–1837)

186. SALISBURY CATHEDRAL. Oil. By John Constable (1776–1837)

ISLAMIC ART

187 EWER. Rock crystal. Egyptian; 10th–12th century

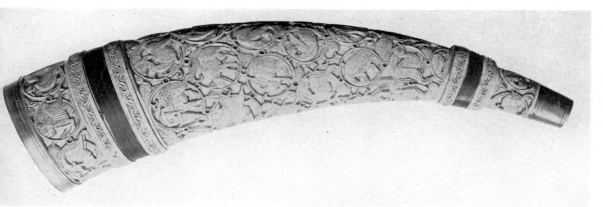

188. PEACOCKS. Silk
tissue. Spanish; 12th
century

189. HORN. Ivory.
Mesopotamian; 10th–
12th century

190. EWER. Brass inlaid with silver. Persian; 13th century

191. CASKET. Ivory. Spanish; 10th century

192. BOWL. Painted earthenware. Persian; early 13th century

193. VASE. Earthenware. Syrian;
14th century

194. MOSQUE LAMP. Enamelled glass.
Syrian; about 1313

195. BOWL. Earthenware.
Persian; second half of the
12th century

196. PULPIT. Inlaid wood. Cairo; last quarter of the 15th century

197. DISH. Earthenware.
Turkish; mid 16th
century

198. JUG. Silver-gilt. Turkish; 16th century

199. PANEL. Silk velvet. Persian; about 1600

200. PANEL OF TILES. Painted and glazed earthenware. Persian; early 17th century

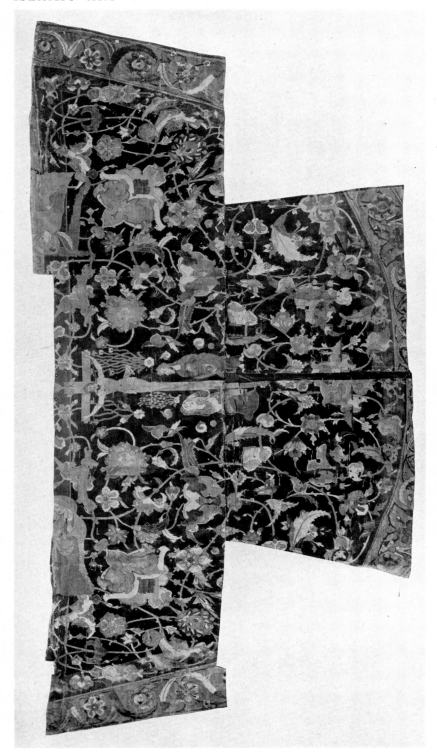

201. THE SAFAWID COPE. Knotted silk pile. Persian; early 17th century

203. CARPET. Woollen pile. Caucusus; 17th century

202. SILK TISSUE. Gold and silver thread. Persian; late 16th century

204. THE CHELSEA CARPET (DETAIL). Woollen pile. Persian; 16th century

205. THE ARDABIL CARPET (DETAIL). Woollen pile. Persian; 1540

206. HEAD OF A HORSE. Jade. Chinese; Han dynasty

207. WINE VESSEL. Bronze. Chinese;
Shang dynasty

208. CAULDRON. Bronze. Chinese;
Shang dynasty

209. BOWL. Celadon. Korean; 11th–12th century

210. VASE. Porcellanous stoneware. Chinese; Sung dynasty

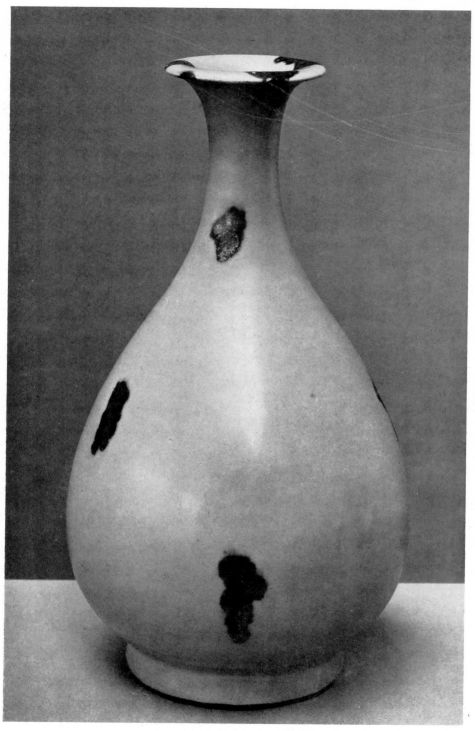

211. BOTTLE. Celadon. Chinese; Sung dynasty

212. DISH. Porcelain. Chinese;
late 14th century

213. JAR. Porcelain. Chinese;
Ming dynasty

214. BOWL. Earthenware. Japanese; early 18th century

215. THE GREAT WAVE OFF KANAZAWA. Colour print. By Hokusai. Japanese: 1823–29

216. THE THRONE OF THE EMPEROR CH'IEN LUNG. Carved lacquer.
Chinese; mid 18th century

217. IMPERIAL DRAGON ROBE. Silk, tapestry-woven. Chinese; reign of K'ang Hsi

218. KUAN YIN. Wood painted and gilt. Chinese; Sung dynasty

INDIAN ART

219. HEAD OF THE BUDDHA. Lime composition. North-west India. 3rd–4th
century A.D.

220. THE SANCHI TORSO. Sandstone. Central India; late 5th–6th century A.D.

222. SIVA, LORD OF THE DANCE. Bronze. Madras; 11th century

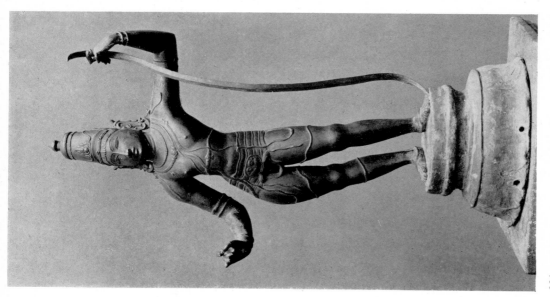

221. RAMA WITH THE BOW. Bronze. Madras; 14th century

223. BEDSPREAD. Cotton embroidered in silk. South Indian; about 1700

224. A MAIDEN AWAITING HER LOVER. Tempera painting. Kangra school; early 19th century

225. THE THREE YOUNGER SONS OF SHAH JAHAN. Tempera painting. Mughal School; about 1635

Descriptive Notes on the Plates

EARLY MEDIAEVAL ART

1 LEAF OF A MARRIAGE DIPTYCH. Ivory. Roman; late 4th century A.D. H. 11⅝ in., W. 4¾ in.   212–1865

2 PANEL. Tapestry-woven in silk, wool and linen. Egyptian; 4th–5th century A.D. 3¾ in. square.
334–1887

3 HERMES. Roundel of looped woollen pile on linen. Egyptian; 4th–5th century A.D. Diameters, 15 in. and 17 in.   T.201–1926

4 THE MIRACLES OF CHRIST. Ivory relief. Early Christian (perhaps Italian); probably 5th century. H. 12 in. W. 7¾ in.   A.47 & a–1926

5 A WINGED MONSTER (SENMURV). Silk tissue. Persian (Sassanian); 6th–7th century. H. 14 in. W. 20¼ in.   8579–1863

6 HERO AND LION. Silk tissue. Alexandrian or Syrian; 6th–7th century. H. 15 in. W. 17 in.   7036–1860

7 THE EASBY CROSS. Fragments of a cross from Easby Church, Richmond, Yorkshire. Sandstone. English; late 7th or early 8th century.
Portions: H. 17½ in., W. 10½ in., D. 6 in.   A.88–1930
H. 19½ in., W. 11¼ in., D. 5½ in.   A.9–1931
H. 18½ in., W. 12½ in., D. 7⅝ in.   A.10–1931

8 THE FILLING OF THE WATER POTS IN THE MIRACLE OF CANA. Ivory relief. Early Christian (Alexandrian); 6th century. H. 4½ in., W. 3⅝ in.
A.1–1921

9 THE EASBY CROSS. Detail.   A.88–1930

10 THE VIRGIN AND CHILD WITH ST. JOHN AND ST. ZACHARIAS. Ivory reliefs. Carolingian; 9th century. H. 15 in., W. 10½ in.   138–1866

11 THE VEROLI CASKET. Ivory reliefs on wood. Byzantine; 8th–10th century. H. 4½ in., L. 15¾ in., W. 6 in.   216–1865

12 HOLY WATER BUCKET (the Basilewski Situla). Ivory. Made perhaps at Milan or possibly Reichenau; about 980. H. 6¼ in.   A.18–1933

13 RELIQUARY CROSS. Walrus ivory mounted on wood covered with gold, filigree work and cloisonné enamels. English; about 1000. H. 7½ in.   7943–1862

14 THE SION GOSPELS BOOK-COVER. Beechwood overlaid with gold enriched with cloisonné enamels and precious stones. North French or German; late 10th–12th century. H. 10 in.   567–1893

15 HEAD OF A PASTORAL STAFF. Ivory. English; 11th–12th century. H. 4¾ in.   218–1865

16 THE VIRGIN AND CHILD. Ivory statuette. Byzantine; 10th–11th century. H. 12¾ in.   702–1884

17 THE GLOUCESTER CANDLESTICK. Gilt bell-metal. English; about 1110. H. 23 in.   7649–1861

18 THE ADORATION OF THE MAGI. Relief in whalebone. English; beginning of the 12th century. H. 14¼ in.   142–1866

19 ST. JOHN THE BAPTIST, WITH ST. PHILIP, ST. STEPHEN, ST. ANDREW AND ST. THOMAS. Pierced ivory relief. Byzantine; 11th or 12th century. H. 9¼ in., W. 5¼ in.   215–1866

20 THE DEPOSITION. Ivory relief. Spanish; 11th–12th century. H. 8⅜ in., W. 4⅝ in.   3–1872

21 EWER. Gilt bronze with niello and silver. Mosan; early 13th century. H. 7⅜ in.   1471–1870

22 THE ELTENBERG RELIQUARY. Copper-gilt and enamelled, with carvings in walrus ivory. German (Cologne); second half of the 12th century. H. 21½ in.
7650–1861

23 A LEAF FROM A PSALTER OR BOOK OF THE GOSPELS. Illuminated manuscript. English (School of Bury St. Edmunds); first half of the 12th century. H. 15¾ in., W. 11¾ in.   816–1894

24 THE ANNUNCIATION. Miniature mosaic. Byzantine; 13th–14th century. H. 5¼ in., W. 3¼ in.
7231–1860

NORTHERN GOTHIC

25 SCENES FROM THE PASSION. Ivory. French; end of the 13th century. H. 12¾ in., W. 9½ in.   211–1865

26 CHRIST ENTHRONED. Embroidery in silk and metal thread on silk. English; early 14th century. H. 3 ft. 3⅜ in., W. 16⅜ in.   T.337–1921

27 THE CLARE CHASUBLE. Embroidery in gilt thread and silk on satin. English; second half of the 13th century. H. 3 ft. 11 in.   673–1864

28 THE STUDLEY BOWL. Silver-gilt. English; late 14th century. H. 5⅝ in.   M.1–1914

29 THE VALENCE CASKET. Copper-gilt, with champlevé enamel. French (Limoges) or possibly English; 1290–96. H. 3¾ in.   4–1865

30 THE TWO MARIES AT THE SEPULCHRE. Ivory. French; mid 14th century. H. 4¼ in.   A.99–1927

31 THE VIRGIN AND CHILD. Sandstone. French; early 14th century. H. 5 ft. 2 in.   A.2–1911

32 THE MÉRODE CUP. Silver-gilt, set with panels of translucent enamel in openwork. Flemish or Burgundian; early 15th century. H. 7 in.   403–1872

33 THE RAMSEY ABBEY CENSER. Silver-gilt. English; second quarter of the 14th century. H. 10⅞ in.
M.268–1923

34 THE VIRGIN AND CHILD. Ivory statuette. French; beginning of the 14th century. H. 14 in.
4685–1858

35 THE REICHENAU CROZIER. Copper-gilt with translucent enamel on silver. South German; dated 1351. H. 20½ in.   7950–1862

36 THE VIRGIN AND CHILD AND CHRIST BLESSING. Ivory diptych. English; early 14th century. H. 8½ in., W. 6⅜ in.   A.545–1910

37 THE SYON COPE. Embroidery in gilt and silver thread and silk on linen. English; early 14th century. L. 9 ft. 8 in., W. 4 ft. 10 in.   83–1864

38 THE WINCHESTER COLLEGE CHAPEL WINDOW (St. John the Evangelist, the Prophet Zephaniah, and St. James the Less). Stained glass. English (probably Oxford); about 1400. H. 11 ft. 7½ in.
4237–1855

39 THE ANGEL OF THE ANNUNCIATION. Painted oak. French; 15th century. H. 3 ft. ½ in. A.10–1914

40 A PAGE FROM THE ST. DENIS MISSAL. Illuminated manuscript. French; about 1370. H. 9½ in.   L.1346–1891

41 THE TROJAN WAR. Tapestry woven in silk and wool on wool. Burgundian (Tournai); about 1470. H. 13 ft. 8 in., W. 12 ft.   6–1887

42 THE DESCENT FROM THE CROSS, THE ENTOMBMENT AND THE RESURRECTION. Tapestry woven in wool, silk, silver and silver-gilt thread on wool. Franco-Burgundian (probably Arras); early 15th century. H. 3 ft. 8 in., W. 9 ft. 11 in. T.1–1921

43 WILD MEN AND ANIMALS. Tapestry woven in wool. Swiss (Basle or Lucerne); mid 15th century. L. 7 ft. 4 in., W. 2 ft. 11 in.   T.117–1937

44 SUSANNA AND THE ELDERS. Tapestry woven in wool and silk on wool. Flemish; about 1500. H. 13 ft. 5 in., W. 11 ft. $\frac{1}{2}$ in.   546–1872

SPANISH GOTHIC

45 THE RETABLE OF ST. GEORGE. Tempera painting and gilding on wood. Spanish (Valencia, possibly by a German artist); about 1400. H. 22 ft., W. 16 ft.   1217–1864

46 DISH. Tin-glazed earthenware with metallic lustre painting (Hispano-Moresque ware). Spanish (Valencia); first half of the 15th century. Diam. 15 in.   1460–1870

47 BOWL. Arms of Portugal. Hispano-Moresque ware. Spanish (Valencia); first half of the 15th century. H. 9 in., Diam. 20 in.   486–1864.

48 CIBORIUM. Silver-gilt. Spanish (Cordova); late 15th century. H. $15\frac{1}{4}$ in.   135–1879

49 CARPET. Knotted wool pile. Spanish; late 16th century. L. 9 ft. 9 in., W. 6 ft. $1\frac{1}{2}$ in.   250–1906

ITALIAN GOTHIC

50 THE ANNUNCIATION. Marble relief, style of Arnolfo di Cambio. Italian (Florentine); about 1290. H. 2 ft. 5 in., L. 4 ft. 2 in.   7563–1861

51 CASKET. Gilt and painted gesso on wood. Italian (Bolognese); second half of the 14th century. H. $9\frac{1}{4}$ in., L. 13 in., W. $6\frac{1}{2}$ in.   351–1864

52 THE ANGEL OF THE ANNUNCIATION. Wood, style of Nino Pisano. Italian (Pisan); mid 14th century. H. 6 ft.   7719–1861

53 THE ARCHANGEL GABRIEL. Marble pier from a pulpit, style of Nicola Pisano. Italian (Pisan); about 1275. H. 3 ft. 2 in., W. $12\frac{1}{2}$ in., D. 8 in.   5800–1859

54 THE CORONATION OF THE VIRGIN. Tempera painting on panel, by Nardo di Cione (fl. 1343–66). Italian (Florentine). H. 3 ft. $10\frac{1}{2}$ in.   C.A.I.104

55 MADONNA AND CHILD. Terracotta, workshop of Ghiberti. Italian (Florentine); about 1425. H. 2 ft. 5 in.   7573–1861

56 CHASUBLE (scenes from the life of the Virgin). Embroidery in silk and silver thread on linen. Italian (Florentine); first quarter of the 15th century. H. 3 ft. $9\frac{1}{2}$ in.   329–1908

57 THE VIRGIN ANNUNCIATE. Terracotta, by the Master of San Martino Pontorme. Italian (Florentine); second quarter of the 15th century. H. 2 ft. 8 in.   8378–1863

58 THE NATIVITY. Gold engraving under glass. North Italian; late 14th century. H. $5\frac{1}{4}$ in., W. $3\frac{1}{2}$ in.   C.2484–1910

59 CHALICE. Silver parcel-gilt with applied openwork and figures cast and chased. Italian (Venetian); about 1480. H. $10\frac{5}{8}$ in.   631–1868

60 THE VIRGIN AND CHILD, WITH KNEELING MEMBERS OF THE GUILD OF SANTA MARIA DELLA MISERICORDIA. Istrian stone, by Bartolomeo Buon (d. 1464). Italian (Venetian); 1451. H. 8 ft. 3 in., W. 6 ft. 10 in.   25–1882

61 THE CONDEMNATION, EXPULSION AND LABOURS OF ADAM AND EVE. Glazed terracotta reliefs mounted on the front of a chest (cassone). Italian (Florentine); second quarter of the 15th century. H. 1 ft. 11 in., L. 5 ft. 6 in.   7613–1861

62 MARRIAGE CHEST. Walnut covered with painted gesso, scenes of falconry. Italian (Florentine); early 15th century. H. $21\frac{1}{2}$ in., L. 4 ft. 8 in.   317–1894

63 DISH. Tin-glazed earthenware (maiolica). Italian (Florentine); about 1450. Diam. $18\frac{1}{2}$ in. 4901–1858

64 DRUG-POT. Tin-glazed earthenware (maiolica). Italian (Florentine); second quarter of the 15th century. H. $14\frac{1}{2}$ in.   2562–1856

ITALIAN RENAISSANCE

65 CHRIST IN THE TOMB WITH ANGELS. Marble relief by Donatello (1386–1466). Italian (Florentine); mid 15th century. H. 2 ft. $7\frac{3}{4}$ in. W. 3 ft. 9 in.   7577–1861

66 THE ASCENSION WITH CHRIST GIVING THE KEYS TO ST. PETER. Marble relief by Donatello (1386–1466). Italian (Florentine); about 1430. H. 1 ft. 4 in., W. 3 ft. 9 in.   7629–1861

67 CUPID OR NARCISSUS. Marble, sometimes ascribed to Michelangelo (1475–1561). Italian (Florentine); first half of the 16th century. H. 3 ft. $5\frac{1}{2}$ in.   7560–1861

68 THE VIRGIN AND CHILD. Marble relief by Desiderio da Settignano (1428–64). Italian (Florentine); third quarter of the 15th century. H. $10\frac{11}{16}$ in., W. $6\frac{1}{2}$ in.   A.84–1927

69 HERCULES WITH THE APPLES OF THE HESPERIDES. Bronze statuette by Bertoldo di Giovanni (1420–1491). Italian (Florentine); last quarter of the 15th century. H. 19 in.   A.76–1910

70 CUPID WITH A FISH. Bronze statuette for a fountain, by Donatello (1386–1466). Italian (Florentine); second quarter of the 15th century. H. 1 ft. 3 in.   475–1864

71 THE LAMENTATION OVER THE DEAD CHRIST. Bronze relief by Donatello. Italian (Florentine); 1450–60. H. 13 in., W. $16\frac{1}{4}$ in.   8552–1863

72 THE CANNING JEWEL. Pearls, diamonds, rubies, enamel and gold. Italian (Tuscan?); late 16th century. H. 4 in., W. $2\frac{3}{4}$ in.   M.2697–1931

73 A SLAVE. Model in wax by Michelangelo (1475–1564). Italian (Florentine); about 1516. H. $6\frac{1}{2}$ in.   4117–1854

74 THE ARMS OF KING RENÉ OF ANJOU. Enamelled terracotta by Luca della Robbia (1399–1482). Italian (Florentine); 1460–70. Diam. 11 ft.   6740–1860

75 THE VIRGIN WITH THE LAUGHING CHILD. Terracotta, by Antonio Rossellino (1427–78). Italian (Florentine); about 1465. H. 1 ft. 7 in.   4495–1858

76 GIOVANNI CHELLINI. Marble bust by Antonio Rossellino (1427–78). Italian (Florentine); signed and dated 1456. H. 1 ft. 8 in.   7671–1861

77 THE VIRGIN AND CHILD. Tempera painting by Carlo Crivelli (1430?–95). Italian (Venetian). H 18½ in., W. 13½ in.   492–1882

78 ALTARPIECE. Marble, by Andrea Ferucci (1465–1526). Italian (Florentine); about 1495. H. 12 ft., W. 9 ft.   6742–1859

79 CHRIST LED FROM JUDGMENT. Relief in red wax by Giovanni Bologna (1529–1608). Italian (Florentine); about 1575. H. 1 ft. 7 in., W. 2 ft. 5 in.   330–1879

80 AN ALLEGORY OF DISCORD. Stucco relief by Francesco di Giorgio Martini (1439–1502). Italian (Sienese); last quarter of the 15th century. H. 19½ in., W. 26½ in.   251–1876

81 WARRIOR ON HORSEBACK. Bronze statuette by Andrea Briosco, called Il Riccio (1470–1532). Italian (Paduan); late 15th or early 16th century. H. 13¼ in.   A.88–1910

82 SATYR AND SATYRESS. Bronze group by Andrea Briosco, called Il Riccio (1470–1532). Italian (Paduan); about 1512. H. 10½ in.   A.8–1949

83 MARRIAGE CHEST. Gilt gesso decorated with paintings of the Arrival of the Queen of Sheba, and Solomon and the Queen of Sheba, by Francesco di Giorgio Martini (1439–1502). Italian (Sienese); about 1475. H. 3 ft. 3 in., W. 6 ft. 3 in.   W.68–1925

84 ALTAR CROSS AND CANDLESTICKS. Crystal, silver-gilt and enamel, set with stones. Said to have been made by Valerio Belli of Vicenza (1468–1546) for Francis I of France. Italian; about 1520. H. (cross) 32¼ in.   757–1864, M.61 & a–1920

85 PAGE FROM AN ILLUMINATED MANUSCRIPT. Petrarch's Sonnets and Triumphs. North Italy; about 1470. H. 9 in., W. 6 in.   L.101–1947

86 THE MIRACULOUS DRAUGHT OF FISHES. Sized colour on paper. Cartoon for tapestry by Raphael (1483–1520). Italian (Rome); 1515. H. 8 ft. 6 in., W. 10 ft. 5½ in.   Lent by H.M. the King

87 THE ADORATION OF THE MAGI. Miniature shrine, enamelled gold. Spanish; 16th century. Diam. 3⅓ in.   M.550–1910

88 THE MARTELLI MIRROR. Bronze, gold and silver. Italian (Florentine); early 16th century. Diam. 7½ in.   8717–1863

89 MAY. Enamelled terracotta plaque, by Luca della Robbia (1399–1482). Italian (Florentine); 1440–45. Diam. 1 ft. 10½ in.   7636–1861

90 PLATE. Tin-glazed earthenware (maiolica), painted by Giovanni Maria. Italian (Castel Durante); about 1515. Diam. 10¼ in.   C.151–1929

91 CHIMNEY-PIECE. Sandstone, by Desiderio da Settignano (1428–64). Italian (Florentine); mid 15th century. H. 8 ft. 6 in., W. 12 ft.   5896–1859

92 THE VIRGIN AND CHILD WITH ANGELS. Marble relief by Agostino di Duccio (1418–80?). Italian (Florentine); about 1460. H. 22 in.   A.14–1926

93 HEAD OF A NEGRESS. Marble ('Verde di prato'). Italian (Florentine); late 16th century. H. 11¼ in.   A.4–1941

94 HENRY VII (r. 1485–1509). Bust in painted and gilded terracotta, by Pietro Torrigiano (1472–1528); Italian (Florentine); early 16th century. H. 3 ft.   A.49–1935

NORTHERN RENAISSANCE

95 RUSTIC SPORTS. Tapestry woven in wool and silk on wool. Flemish (Tournai); early 16th century. 11 ft. 2¼ in. square.   5668a–1859

96 A CASTLE WITH THE ADORATION OF THE MAGI. Morse; silver-gilt with enamels and pearls. French; late 15th century. Diam. 5 in.   394–1872

97 ST. MARGARET IN PRISON. Stained glass (yellow stain and grisaille). Flemish (probably Antwerp); 1520–30. Diam. 8¼ in.   C.351–1930

98 THE RESURRECTION. Tapestry woven in silk and wool, silver and silver-gilt thread on wool. Flemish (probably Brussels); first quarter of the 16th century. H. 8 ft. 4½ in.   T.139–1921

99 THE CHRIST CHILD BLESSING. Bronze statuette, perhaps by Pankraz Labenwolf (1492–1563). German (Nuremberg); early 16th century. H. 1 ft. 7 in.   411–1854

100 SIDEBOARD. Carved and inlaid walnut. French; about 1560. H. 4 ft. 7 in., L. 3 ft. 10 in.   7219–1860

101 THE VIRGIN AND CHILD. Boxwood statuette by Veit Stoss (1447–1533). German; first decade of the 16th century. H. 8⅝ in.   646–1893

102 MARY SALOME AND ZEBEDEE. Limewood carving by Tilman Riemenschneider (1460–1531). German; about 1506. H. 3 ft. 11 in.   110–1878

103 COLUMBINE CUP. Qualifying cup for the rank of master of the Goldsmith's Guild of Nuremberg. Silver. German; about 1572. H. 8½ in.   150–1872

104 AN ANGEL WITH A CANDLESTICK. Limewood carving by Tilman Riemenschneider (1460–1531). German; early 16th century. H. 2 ft. 1 in.   A.17–1912

105 TRIPTYCH. The Annunciation, flanked by Louis XII of France and his Queen, Anne of Brittany. Painted enamel on copper. French (Limoges); about 1500. W. 19⅛ in.   552–1877

106 CLAUDE, QUEEN OF FRANCIS I OF FRANCE. Painted enamel by Léonard Limousin. French (Limoges); about 1550. H. 12⅝ in.   C.2416–1910

107 MARIE DE'MEDICI (1573–1642). Black and red chalk drawing by Sir Peter Paul Rubens (1577–1640). Flemish; about 1617. H. 12½ in., W. 9¾ in.   D.906–1900

108 BOOK COVER. Once the property of Henrietta Maria, Queen of Charles I. Enamelled gold. South German; about 1600. H. 3¾ in.   736–1864

CONTINENTAL ART

109 PORTRAIT OF AN ENGLISHMAN (Mr. Baker?). Marble bust by Gian Lorenzo Bernini (1598–1680). Italian (Rome); about 1639. H. 32 in.   A.63–1921

110 NEPTUNE AND GLAUCUS. Marble fountain group by Gian Lorenzo Bernini (1598–1680). Italian (Rome); about 1622. H. 6 ft. 1 in.   A.18–1950

111 THE VIRGIN OF SORROWS. Bust in painted wood, probably by Pedro de Mena (1628–88). Spanish; mid 17th century. H. 16¾ in. 1284–1871

112 CHARLES II (1630–85). Marble bust signed by Honoré Pelle. French; 1684. H. 4 ft. 3 in. 239–1881

113 THE JUDGMENT OF SOLOMON. Bowl of a standing dish (tazza). Silver, by Adam van Vianen (d. 1627). Dutch; Utrecht mark for 1612. H. 6½ in. Diam. 8 in. 2125–1855

114 COMMODE. Marquetry of brass, ivory, ebony and tortoiseshell in the manner of A. C. Boulle. French: late Louis XIV (early 18th century). H. 2 ft. 7⅜ in., L. 3 ft. 11¾ in. 372–1901

115 DIANA. Boxwood statuette by Leonhard Kern (1588–1663). German; mid 17th century. H. 9 in. A.1–1922

116 SEATED GIRL. Lead statuette by Adriaen de Vries (1560–1627). North Netherlandish; first quarter of the 17th century. H. 1 ft. 4 in. A.2–1946

117 A HUNT PICNIC. Porcelain, modelled by Franz Anton Bustelli (fl. 1754–63). German (Nymphenburg); 1759–60. H. 10¾ in. C.21–1946

118 A BACCHANTE. Terracotta, by Joseph Marin (1759–1834). French; dated 1786. H. 11½ in. 890–1882

119 LOUIS XV AS APOLLO. Terracotta bust by Lambert Sigisbert Adam (1700–59). French; about 1741. H. 3 ft. ¾ in. A.17–1947

120 COVERED BEAKER. Glass, engraved by Gottfried Spiller in Berlin. German (made at Potsdam); about 1700. H. 8½ in. 520–1872

121 LEDA AND THE SWAN. Biscuit porcelain modelled by Étienne-Maurice Falconet from a design by François Boucher (1703–70). French (Sèvres); about 1765. H. 13 in. 382–1874

122 AUTUMN. Porcelain group modelled by J. J. Kaendler (1706–75). German (Meissen); about 1765. H. 11 in. C.209–1921

123 MADAME DE POMPADOUR. Oil painting by François Boucher (1703–70). French; signed and dated 1758. H. 28½ in., W. 22½ in. 487–1882

124 VOLTAIRE (1694–1778). Marble bust by Jean Antoine Houdon (1741–1828). French; dated 1781. H. 20 in. A.24–1948

125 WRITING CABINET AND DRESSING-TABLE (Secrétaire-Toilette). Marquetry of various woods, ormolu mounts. French; about 1775. H. 3 ft. 5 in. W. 2 ft. 9 in., D. 1 ft. 8 in. 1043–1882

126 UPRIGHT SECRÉTAIRE. Marquetry of various woods, ormolu mounts, probably by David Roentgen (1743–1807). Franco-German; period of Louis XVI (end of the 18th century). H. 5 ft., W. 3 ft. 1107–1882

127 THE DUKE OF REICHSTADT (1811–32), Son of Napoleon I. Portrait miniature by Jean Baptiste Isabey (1767–1855). French; about 1820. H. 10¼ in. W. 8 in. P.40–1948

128 ALEXANDRINE D'ETIOLLES. Daughter of Madame de Pompadour. Marble bust by Jacques Saly (1717–54). French; about 1750. H. 19 in. 8510–1863

129 COMMODE. Marquetry with brass mounts and marble top, by David Roentgen (1743–1807). Franco-German (Neuwied-am-Rhein); 1780–90. H. 2 ft. 10½ in., W. 4 ft. 5 in., D. 2 ft. 2½ in. W.51–1948

130 RIVER-GOD. Terracotta, signed by Claude Michel called Clodion (1738–1814). French; end of the 18th century. H. 13¾ in., L. 15¼ in. 1064–1884

ENGLISH ART 1500–1660

131 THE GREAT BED OF WARE. Oak, carved, painted and inlaid. English; last quarter of the 16th century. L. 11 ft., W. 11 ft. W.47–1931

132 TABLE DESK. Painted leather; badges and arms of Henry VIII and Catherine of Arragon. English; about 1525. L. 16 in., D. 11½ in. W.29–1932

133 STANDING LIVERY CUPBOARD. Oak. English; about 1500. H. 5 ft. 4½ in., W. 4 ft. 1½ in. W.15–1912

134 THE VYVYAN SALT. Silver-gilt, set with painted glass panels. English; London hall-mark for 1592–3. H. 15¾ in. M.273–1925

135 THE MOSTYN SALT. Silver-gilt. English; London hall-mark for 1586–7. H. 16⅛ in. 146–1886

136 THE HOWARD GRACE CUP. Ivory mounted in silver-gilt. English; London hall-mark for 1525–6. H. 12 in. M.2680–1931

137 QUEEN ELIZABETH (1533–1603). Unfinished portrait miniature by Isaac Oliver (d. 1617). English; about 1600. H. 2⅜ in., W. 2½ in. P.8–1940

138 THE ARMADA JEWEL. Relief portrait of Queen Elizabeth (1533–1603) in gold set with diamonds and rubies. By Nicholas Hilliard? (1547–1619). English; about 1588. H. 2¾ in. M.81–1935

139 ANNE OF CLEVES. (1515–57). Portrait miniature by Hans Holbein (1497?–1543). English; about 1539. Diam. 1¾ in. P.153–1910

140 MRS PEMBERTON (d. 1576). Portrait miniature by Hans Holbein (1497?–1543). English; about 1540. Diam. 2⅛ in. P.40–1935

141 PANELLED ROOM. Oak inlaid; from Sizergh Castle, Westmoreland. English; about 1575. H. 12 ft. 6 in. 3–1891

142 YOUNG MAN AMONG FLAMES. Portrait miniature by Nicholas Hilliard (1547–1619). English; end of the 16th century. H. 2⅝ in., W. 2 in. P.5–1917

143 GOBLET. Made in the glass-house of Jacopo Verzilini, engraved with diamond-point, perhaps by Anthony de Lyde. English; dated 1581. H. 8⅛ in. C.523–1936

144 YOUNG MAN AMONG ROSES. Portrait miniature by Nicholas Hilliard (1547–1619). English; about 1588. H. 5⅜ in., W. 2¾ in. P.163–1910

145 REBECCAH AT THE WELL. Plate, silver-gilt and engraved. English; London hall-mark for 1573–4. Diam. 10 in. M.55c–1946

146 THE BRADFORD TABLE CARPET. Embroidery, silk on linen canvas. English; late 16th century. L. 13 ft., W. 5 ft., 9 in. T.134–1928

147 COURT CUPBOARD. Oak, carved and joined. English; early 17th century. H. 3 ft. 10½ in. W. 3 ft. 11 in. W.61–1950

148 RICHARD SACKVILLE (1589–1624), THIRD EARL OF DORSET. Portrait miniature by Isaac Oliver (d. 1617). English; signed and dated 1616. H. 9¼ in., W. 6 in. 721–1882

149 THE FLIGHT INTO EGYPT. Tapestry-woven panel, silk, wool, silver and silver-gilt thread on wool. English (Sheldon); late 16th century. H. 8 in., L. 11⅛ in. T.85–1913

150 THE GODS DISCOVERING THE AMOURS OF MARS AND VENUS. Tapestry, silk, wool, silver and silver-gilt thread on wool. English (Mortlake); about 1625. H. 15 ft., W. 18 ft. 9 in. 1105–1898

151 THE ADORATION OF THE SHEPHERDS. Embroidered picture, silk, silver and silver-gilt thread on linen, by Edmund Harrison, embroiderer to Charles I. English; signed and dated 1637. L. 3 ft. 7 in., W. 2 ft. 4½ in. T.147–1930

ENGLISH DECORATIVE ARTS FROM 1660

152 THE STONING OF ST. STEPHEN. Relief carving in limewood and lancewood by Grinling Gibbons (1648–1722). English; late 17th or early 18th century. H. 6 ft. ½ in., W. 4 ft. 4¾ in. 446–1898

153 THE EARLIEST DATED TEAPOT. Silver. English. London hall-mark for 1670–71. H. 13½ in. 02640

154 A HERALD. Black chalk drawing on toned paper by Sir Peter Lely (1618–80). English; late 17th century. H. 19½ in., W. 9⅞ in. E.I.D.2166

155 CLOCK. Engraved silver case, signed 'Edward Webbe in Church Stoke'. English; 1676. H. 15½ in., W. 6¼ in. M.45–1946

156 PILGRIM-BOTTLE. Silver, engraved with the arms of General Charles Churchill (d. 1714); maker's mark of Pierre Platel. English (London); 1702–14. H. 15⅞ in. M.854–1927

157 FIREDOG. Enamelled brass. English; second half of the 17th century. H. 24½ in. 416–1905

158 THE ASHBURNHAM GARNITURE (one of three pieces). Silver-gilt; maker's mark H.M. crowned. English; London hall-mark for 1675–6. H. 13½ in. M.46–1914

159 THE STERNE CUP. Silver-gilt. English; London hall-mark for 1673–4. H. 7¾ in. M.103–1925

160 SALVER. Silver-gilt; maker's mark of Thomas Farren. English; London hall-mark for 1733–4. W. 14⅞ in. M.3–1926

161 CABINET. Walnut with marquetry. English; about 1700. H. 7 ft. 10 in., W. 4 ft. 9 in. W.136–1928

162 CHINOISERIES. Tapestry woven in silk and wool on wool; signed by John Vanderbank (1694?–1739). English (Soho); early 18th century. H. 10 ft. 1 in., W. 9 ft. 3 in. T.362–1910

163 SIDE-TABLE. Carved and gilt wood, designed by Henry Flitcroft (1697–1769), the top of scagliola (composition) made at Leghorn. English; 1725–6. H. 2 ft. 9 in., W. 4 ft. 9 in. W.6–1933

164 CHEST. Carved and gilt gesso. English; about 1720. H. 2 ft. 7 in., W. 4 ft. 9 in. W.33–1948

165 THE GARRICK FURNITURE. Japanned wood; from David Garrick's villa at Hampton. Probably made by Chippendale, Haig and Co. English (London); about 1775. Bed H. 8 ft., L. 6 ft. 6½ in. W.70–1916

166 THE KIMBOLTON CABINET. Rosewood and satinwood veneer with inlaid decoration and gilt bronze mounts. Designed by Robert Adam for the Duchess of Manchester, to receive eleven pieces of marble mosaic. English; 1771. The mosaics Italian (Florentine), signed by Baccio Cappelli and dated 1709. H. 6 ft. 1½ in. W.43–1949

167 LIBRARY TABLE. Carved mahogany with gilt brass mounts. English; about 1755–60. H. 2 ft. 7 in., W. 5 ft. 3 in. W.56–1948

168 COMMODE. Mahogany with marquetry and ormolu mounts, made by John Cobb, upholsterer to George III. English (London); about 1775. H. 2 ft. 10½ in., L. 3 ft. 8 in. W.30–1937

169 SETTEE. Carved mahogany, 'Ribband Back' design from Chippendale's *Director*. English; about 1755. L. 4 ft. 2 in. W.64–1935

170 BEDSTEAD. Wood with japanned decoration, from Badminton House, Gloucestershire; probably made by Thomas Chippendale. English; 1750–55. H. 12 ft. 6 in., L. 8 ft. 6 in. W.143–1921

171 THE NEWDIGATE CENTREPIECE. Silver, by Paul Lamerie. English; London hall-mark for 1743–4. H. 9⅞ in. M.149–1919

172 PUNCH-POT. White salt-glazed stoneware with decoration in polychrome enamels. English (Staffordshire), about 1765. H. 7⅜ in. C.81–1938

173 TEAPOT. Cream-coloured earthenware printed in red, perhaps by John Sadler of Liverpool. English (Burslem, Josiah Wedgwoods factory); about 1765–70. H. 5⅜ in. 2333 & a–1901

174 THE CARPENTER. Porcelain figure. English (Chelsea); about 1755. H. 7¾ in. 2923–1901

175 THE MUSIC LESSON. Porcelain group after a painting by François Boucher (1703–70). English (Chelsea); about 1765. H. 16 in. Schreiber 197

176 SIR GEORGE SAVILE (1726–84). Marble bust by Joseph Nollekens (1737–1823). English; signed and dated 1784. H. 30½ in. A.16–1942

177 MODEL FOR THE MONUMENT TO JOHN, DUKE OF ARGYLL, IN WESTMINSTER ABBEY. Terracotta, by Louis François Roubiliac (1705–1762). English; signed and dated 1745. H. 34½ in. 21–1888

178 IN A SHOREHAM GARDEN. Water-colour and gouache by Samuel Palmer (1805–81). H. 11 in., W. 8¾ in. P.32–1926

179 SATAN AROUSING THE REBEL ANGELS. Water-colour drawing by William Blake (1757–1827), signed and dated 1808. H. 20½ in., W. 15⅜ in. F.A.697

180 GLOUCESTER, 1840. Water-colour by Peter de Wint (1784–1847). H. 17⅞ in., W. 24⅝ in. P.62–1921

181 LANDSCAPE WITH RIVER AND CATTLE. Water-colour signed by John Sell Cotman (1782–1842). H. 8⅜ in., W. 12⅜ in. 93–1894

182 ENTRANCE TO THE MALL, SPRING GARDENS. Water-colour drawing by Thomas Rowlandson (1756–1827). H. 13¼ in., W. 18¼ in. P.110–1931

183 THE PAINTER'S TWO DAUGHTERS. Oil painting by Thomas Gainsborough, R.A. (1727–88). H. 16 in., W. 25 in. F.9

184 KIRKSTALL ABBEY, YORKSHIRE—EVENING. Water-colour by Thomas Girtin (1775–1802). H. 12 in., W. 20½ in. 405–1885

185 THE HAY WAIN. Study in oils for the picture now in the National Gallery, by John Constable, R.A. (1776–1837). H. 4 ft. 6 in., W. 6 ft. 2 in.   987–1900

186 SALISBURY CATHEDRAL FROM THE BISHOP'S GROUNDS. Oil painting by John Constable, R.A. (1776–1837). Signed and dated 1823. H. 34 in., W. 43½ in.   F.A.33

ISLAMIC ART

187 EWER. Rock crystal. Egyptian; 10th–12th century. H. 8½ in.   7904–1862

188 PEACOCKS. Silk tissue. Spanish; 12th century. H. 13 in., W. 9½ in.   828–1894

189 HORN. Carved ivory, probably Mesopotamian; 10th–12th century. L. 25 in.   7953–1862

190 EWER. Brass inlaid with silver. Persian; early 13th century. H. 17¼ in., W. 8¼ in.   381–1897

191 CASKET. Carved ivory with engraved silver mounts. Spanish; 10th century (the mounts 17th century). H. 8½ in., L. 10½ in.   10–1866

192 BOWL. Earthenware painted in black and blue. Persian (Kashan); early 13th century. Diam. 7¾ in.   C.721–1909

193 VASE. Earthenware. Syrian; 14th century. H. 15 in.   483–1864

194 MOSQUE LAMP. Enamelled glass. Syrian (Damascus); about 1313. H. 11⅜ in.   580–1875

195 BOWL. Earthenware with design in black slip under a clear glaze. Persian; second half of the 12th century. Diam. 8⅛ in.   C.282–1938

196 PULPIT (MIMBAR). Wood inlaid with ivory and ebony. Presented to a mosque in Cairo by the Mamluk Sultan Kait Bay. Egyptian; 1468–96. H. 24 ft.   1050–1869

197 DISH. Earthenware, painted in three shades of blue. Turkish (Isnik); mid 16th century. H. 1½ in., Diam. 12⅞ in.   713–1902

198 JUG. Silver-gilt. Turkish; 16th century (cover later). H. 6¼ in.   158–1894

199 PERSIAN PARADISE (DETAIL). Silk velvet woven with gold and silver thread. Persian; about 1600. W. 2 ft. 6 in.   T.226–1923

200 PANEL. Painted and glazed earthenware tiles; from a pavilion of the Royal Palace, Isfahan. Persian; early 17th century. H. 3 ft. 7 in.   139–1891

201 COPE, cut later to a dalmatic. Knotted silk pile enriched with silver and silver-gilt. Persian; early 17th century. H. 4 ft. 11 in., W. 7 ft. 9 in.   477–1894

202 SILK TISSUE. Woven in gold and silver thread. Persian; late 16th century. L. 5 ft. 9 in., W. 3 ft. 7 in.   T.9–1915

203 CARPET. Woollen pile on wool. Caucusus or Armenia; 17th century. L. 11 ft. 6 in., W. 6 ft. 5 in.   T.420–1906

204 THE 'CHELSEA' CARPET (Detail). Woollen pile on wool. Persian; 16th century. L. 17 ft. 8 in., W. 9 ft. 8 in.   589–1890

205 THE ARDABIL CARPET (Detail). Woollen pile on wool; from the mosque at Ardabil. Persian; dated 1540. L. 34 ft. 6 in., W. 17 ft. 6 in.   272–1893

FAR EASTERN ART

206 HEAD OF A HORSE. Jade. Chinese; Han dynasty (206 B.C.–220 A.D.). H. 5½ in.   A.16–1935

207 WINE VESSEL (TSUN) IN THE FORM OF AN OWL. Bronze. Chinese; Shang dynasty (1766–1122 B.C.). H. 8¼ in.   M.5–1935

208 CAULDRON (TING). Bronze. Chinese; Shang dynasty (1766–1122 B.C.). H. 8⅜ in.   M.2696–1931

209 BOWL. Ash-grey porcelain with incised decoration under crackled sea-green glaze. Korean; 11th–12th century A.D. Diam. 7¾ in.   C.155–1926

210 VASE. Porcellanous stoneware painted in brownish-black with a cream glaze (Tz'ü-chou ware). Chinese; Sung dynasty (960–1279 A.D.). H. 15 in.   C.68–1935

211 BOTTLE. Porcelain with brown-spotted celadon glaze (Lung-chüan ware). Chinese; Sung dynasty (960–1279). H. 10⅞ in.   C.24–1935

212 DISH. Blue and white porcelain. Chinese; late 14th century. H. 3¼ in., Diam. 18 in.   786–1894

213 JAR. Porcelain with decoration in raised outlines filled with coloured glazes. Chinese; Ming dynasty (1368–1643). H. 14½ in.   C.996–1910

214 BOWL. Earthenware; marked 'Kenzan'. Japanese (Kyoto); early 18th century. Diam. 8 in.   270–1877

215 THE GREAT WAVE OFF KANAZAWA. Colourprint by Hokusai (1760–1849); from 'The Thirty-six Views of Mount Fuji'. Japanese; 1823–9. H. 9¾ in., W. 14⅜ in.   E.4823–1916

216 THE THRONE OF THE EMPEROR CH'IEN LUNG (r. 1736–95). Carved red lacquer. Chinese; mid 18th century. H. 3 ft. 11 in., W. 4 ft. 1½ in.   W.399–1922

217 TWELVE-SYMBOL IMPERIAL DRAGON ROBE. Blue and white silk, tapestry-woven. Chinese; reign of K'ang Hsi (1662–1722).   T.189–1948

218 KUAN YIN (Goddess of Mercy). Wood, painted and gilt. Chinese; Sung dynasty (960–1279 A.D.). H. 3 ft. 9 in.   A.7–1935

INDIAN ART

219 HEAD OF THE BUDDHA. Lime composition. Gandhara, north-west India; 3rd–4th century A.D. H. 11 in., W. 7¼ in., D. 7⅞ in.   I.M.3–1931

220 TORSO OF A BODDHISATTVA. Red sandstone. Sanchi (Central India); late Gupta period, 5th–6th century A.D. H. 2 ft. 10 in., W. 15½ in.   I.M.184–1910

221 RAMA WITH THE BOW. Bronze. South Indian (Madras Presidency); 14th century. H. 2 ft. 6 in.   I.M.71–1927

222 SIVA, LORD OF THE DANCE. Bronze. South Indian (Madras Presidency); 11th century. H. 2 ft. 8 in.   I.M.71–1935

223 BEDSPREAD. Cotton embroidered in coloured silks; made for the Western markets. South Indian; about 1700. L. 11 ft. 8 in., W. 8 ft. 4 in.   29–1889

224 A MAIDEN AWAITING HER LOVER IN THE FOREST. Tempera painting. Pahari, Kangra school; early 19th century. H. 11⅛ in., W. 7⅞ in.   I.M.157–1914

225 THE THREE YOUNGER SONS OF SHAH JEHAN. Tempera painting by Balchand. Mughal school; about 1635. H. 10½ in., W. 7⅞ in.   I.M.13–1925

Wt. 3796   K56 + 8   S.O. Code No. 29–1589–1*

Printed in Great Britain under the authority of H.M. Stationery Office
by W. S. Cowell Ltd, Butter Market, Ipswich